On a Hook Behind the Door

Fran Graham

On a Hook Behind the Door

Acknowledgements

Some of the poems in this collection have been previously published: A Grandmother Keeps in Touch, *Twilight Musings* (International Library of Poetry); Alzheimer's, *Poetrix*; Waiting (from Bipolar Cycle), *Famous Reporter*; Canine Reserve, *A Net of Hands* (FAW Tas); Carpet Ride, *RePUBlic Readings*; Celebrating the Effect, *Ask the Rain* (Poets Union); Cemetery (Maria Island), *Famous Reporter*; Chinese Translation, *The International Who's Who of Poetry* (The International Library of Poetry); Chronic Fatigue Syndrome, *Philomel & Wattlebird* (FAW Tas); Cottesloe: An Impromptu for Carol Pettit, *A Net of Hands* (FAW Tas); Father, *fourW thirteen* (FourW Press); It's a Small World, *Philomel & Wattlebird* (FAW Tas); Menopause, *Famous Reporter*; Outback, *Sun and Sleet* (Poets Union), *Forever Spoken* (International Library of Poetry); Recycled, *Poetrix*; Rainy Day Sonnet, *Songs of Honour* (Noble House); Resurrection, *Poetrix*; Spring Sonnet, *A Net of Hands* (FAW Tas); Strained, *Red Jelly* (Tasmanian Arts Council); The Birthday Party, *australianreader.com*; The kookaburras, *A Net of Hands* (FAW Tas); The Tao of Loss, *Running through the Stars* (FAW Tas); Seeing Sam, *Running through the Stars* (FAW Tas); Then Let Her Slip Away, *Famous Reporter*; Tissue Test, *RePUBlic Readings*; Tom, *A Net of Hands* (FAW Tas); Tryst, *From the Anabranch* (Poets Union)

For Lisa, Carey, Gene and Terese

On a Hook Behind the Door
ISBN 978 1 74027 713 6
Copyright © Fran Graham 2011

First published 2011
This edition published 2015

GINNINDERRA PRESS
PO Box 3461 Port Adelaide SA 5015
www.ginninderrapress.com.au

Contents

A Grandmother Keeps in Touch	7
Alzheimer's	8
At My Window	9
At the Cabin	10
Bipolar Cycle	12
Boarding School	17
Canine Reserve	18
Carpet Ride	19
Celebrating the Effect	20
Cemetery (Maria Island)	22
Coming Down With Something	23
Contact	24
Chinese Translation	25
Chronic Fatigue Syndrome	26
Cottesloe: An Impromptu for Carol Pettit	27
Father	28
Frail	30
Golden but Tarnished	31
Isobar Pearl	33
It's a Small World	34
Knitting	35
Menopause	37
Mental Illness (Lisa unwell)	40
New Father, My Son	41
Nullarbor Cathedral	44
Opinion Poll	45
Outback	46
Pirates Bay	47
Plastic	48
Recycled	49

Rainy Day Sonnet	50
Resurrection	51
Seeing Sam	53
Speaking With Picasso About His Work	54
Spirited Child	57
Spring Sonnet	58
Strained	59
The Birthday Party	60
The kookaburras	61
The Tao of Loss	62
Then Let Her Slip Away	64
Tissue Test	65
Tom	66
Tryst	67
Valediction	68
Villanelle for the Scotsman	70
Wheels of Fortune	71

A Grandmother Keeps in Touch

I think of you as I post the
picture of the mountain under snow.
Postcards are our lifeline.
I write how we took you there
when you were three days old.
As the van crawled up Pinnacle Road
the snow blew horizontal,
hung delicately from limbs and leaves,
the glare off roadside drifts blinding us.
You slept while we celebrated
this late falling, and your arrival.

Over the phone across the continent
I tell you it's cold here. Yes, you say,
and mention snow. So I promise the card.
I think of you reading it aloud in bed
with your three-year-old imagination
articulating what you know is there
and embellishments that aren't.
When I learn the bits I didn't write
I like them best of all.

Alzheimer's

Bill is on a treadmill getting lost.
Occasionally it stops and lets him off
for a lucid conversation with wife, Mary
or a chat with the neighbours.
Then it's back to the frightened,
sometimes angry, isolation of his world.

He doesn't remember he's had
two heart attacks and almost died.
Or that they've installed a pacemaker as a last resort
but say there's not much they can do.
He forgets it all at times
and says he's never felt better.

In hospital he's adamant
the nurses' station is the Casino.
Mary offers to place a bet.
Oh, no, he says, I never gamble.
The skin of their relationship
is tough with age. She's grateful
he hasn't forgotten who she is.

Bill's understanding dissolves like clouds.
Phantoms decorate his space, spread camouflage,
confusion and an unsound order.
Sam, the dog, is sympathetic.
He's Bill's reliable positioning system
and most effective tranquilliser.
He cries when Bill goes to hospital. Otherwise
he's unfazed that Bill can't remember
that he can't remember.

At My Window

Dawn light pushes back the dark.
Day begins its lazy arrival
unsure of what to wear.

Distant brightness looks promising
but above me
dishwater clouds
lurk like thugs
marring a celebration.

A breeze picks up.
The trees are restless.
Birds behave erratically.
A ginger cat crawls the curb
then disappears
down a side alley.

The clouds are on the move
and blue sky appears
as if my sitting here
disappointed
has helped it remember
it's Christmas Eve.

At the Cabin

Green carpets surround
my dairy palace
snug in the
valley's cleavage,
intimate space.
Creek frogs
croak homage.
Wrens bounce and flit.
At night
the heavens display
their entire shop.
Possums ski down
corrugated slopes.
Wallabies pogo-stick
off into the void.
In the morning
bulbs stand up bravely
against late frost.
Daffodils slowly
don their bonnets
against the sun.
I hear the prelude
to summer's birth
while my heart beats
within the earth.

At night, I sit for hours
variations on an L shape
in my camp chair,
my bottom numb
knee joints complaining
but too warm to move from the fire.

Suddenly the costume fits
and I realise that for years
I misunderstood my role
and played someone else entirely.
Alone now
with no lines to deliver
I am myself
with conviction and ease.

Here
I read four books
in as many days,
chop wood,
mow the lawn,
bird watch
and speak to the cows
while the kettle boils.
I watch Venus rise
and stand back from the edge
of my dreaming.

For supper
I spread peanut butter
on dry bread
then close the fire doors.
Against the solitary plucking
of the banjo frogs
I brush the grass from my clothes
slip off my gumboots
and into bed.

Bipolar Cycle

1. Waiting

I'm trying to make a holiday
out of a mercy dash.
One day I visit you in hospital
and worry,
and the next
I play tourist
and try to relax.

Some days you utter logic
philosophy and wisdom
punctuated by impatience.
On other days you cry,
struggle to name the unbearable
utter your despair.

Yesterday in the garden
I worked so vigorously
I broke Paddy's broom handle
(better it than me)
then stuffed the weeds
along with my fragility
into the wheelie bin.

Today you've asked me
to bring a picnic.
I'm making egg and lettuce
sandwiches sprinkled with
calm, sanity, love
and the desperate hope
that your lithium
will start working soon.

2. Worrying

I'm enjoying staying in the house
you don't want to come home to.
For me there are no ghosts here.
It's peaceful.

I think of you in hospital,
accept your reverse charge calls
half a dozen times a day,
send you my calming energy
when you say you're agitated
and can't get relief,
and I ache with concern.

Each day you become
a little more coherent,
your concentration span
a little longer,
your old sense of humour
a little more visible.

You tell me how much you love me,
how glad you are that I am here,
and a few other things
you've forgotten you told me
the day before.

When I find myself worrying about you
I consciously convert the energy
into willing you well again.
Mothers are good at that.

Twice now I've stepped over
the blood on the carpet
outside the bathroom door
and think of the night you
carved your wrist
compelled, you say,
by a voice inside your head.

I think about births and deaths.
Hope, like incense fills the room.
I breathe deeply.

3. Working at It

Lisa is working hard to stay sane.
Her friend Penny
is trying to find herself.
Together
they go to meditation
the Mystical Minds shop
and McDonalds.

Penny asks why they're doing it.
Lisa says
because it's fun
interesting
and an opportunity to grow.

Penny has a good husband
two degrees
and something missing in her life.

Lisa has it all
but sometimes
loses her mind.

They are wise women
highly educated.

Penny goes to university.
Lisa goes to hospital.

4. Learning to Draw the Line

It's a process of evolution
knowing when to declare
before it's too late
to avoid the crash.
But she's gaining on it.

So when the baby is sick
for six days straight
she says she's had enough.
Dave says he'll take
Manny to work.
To make sure she doesn't cross the line
she stays in bed
until they leave the house.
It's insurance.

She's learning not to
torture herself with
comparisons to other mothers.
She's faced it.
She's not like them.

She spends the morning
sorting her essential oils,
burning incense
and playing reiki music.
She can feel herself
pulling back from the edge.

At the markets
she plays a didgeridoo.
She blows her fear down
the dark hollow of the eucalypt.
The vibration brings good news.
For today she's managed
to stay this side of the line.

Boarding School

Slippers only to be worn in dormitories
the notice said. I pointed out that it was
ambiguous and had several possible meanings.
But that was impertinence
which was anathema
and could result in
a serious number of demerit points.

From the showers,
socks dropped through louvred windows
into the convent courtyard
provided an excuse for invasion of the cloister
if, after doing the dare,
you didn't get out in time.

At end of year when parole was assured
Saint Patrick, centrepiece of the front garden,
held aloft on his sceptre a size 32A bra
and in the V of his raised victory fingers
a half-smoked Rothmans filter tip.

In my dreams I'm often back there.
Happy years of self-discovery
and reckless free flight,
a galaxy of glorious memories,
benign anarchy our only challenge
to the rigours of religion
and caustic cosmic rhetoric.

Canine Reserve

In Jiaxing, dogs hang their hunger
out to dry, sniffing coloured rags
near smouldering fires
and nosing into waste paper.
Febrile with food scent
and chastened by glyphs of illusion
they are passive
in their disappointment.

Throughout this chaotic city
temptations dressed in allure
deceive them. Bits and pieces
litter curb and corner
disguised as signals set to bend
the hard-wired appetite
of bathhouse bitsers.

They follow the wind.
Hope floods their expression like molasses.
To get riled up would be to lose face.
Not many people have pets in China.

Carpet Ride

After a week of psyching myself up
I bow towards Moonah
the floor covering Mecca
and begin the pilgrimage.

I pay homage
at several different shrines
but can't find the mat
with the vibe that hums Nirvana.

Disappointed, I take home
some samples to throw down
against my freshly painted walls
and hope that they'll decide
amongst themselves which
is to be the chosen one.
Chanting 'I am a peaceful soul'
I go to my meditation room
to regain my calm.

On Monday
they'll come to do
the measure and quote.
Perhaps by then
there'll be an obvious volunteer
a flaunter
able to convince me
it won't mind being
walked all over
and really wants to get laid.

Celebrating the Effect

Against the noise of my
impatience I wonder if
you've received my letter yet.

The poem you said you
wrote for me has
made my ego blush.

Flattery is a potent drug.
I am light-headed
not quite responsible.

I want to ring you
but my words would
stagger under the intoxication.

My hope is lit up
waiting, unsure of
what it wants.

In a daydream we
have coffee together and
stir each other's intrigue.

I bite into the chocolate
cake of my longing and
savour the pleasure.

We do not speak.
I lick my lips in a
natural rhythm of caress.

You have taught me
to weather the slow
isolation of waiting.

In the privacy of an
obscure thought I practise
receiving your embrace.

Cemetery (Maria Island)

Inside the fence
all residents dwell underground.
Headstones lean like dominoes
ready to fall,
identities half hidden behind
hard to read script.
No mist or aura
semaphores menace here.
No occult proxy
lurks to loop possession
or lethal riddle round
visitors caring enough
to come in.

There is an ambience
in its runic design,
an isolated force of
eerie, unknown atonement,
a fertile simplicity,
a sharp attraction.

Crypt-like, cobwebs tinsel the pickets,
the surrounding landscape
a mystical concubine
lying close enough to
perhaps hear James Jarvis,
the youngest incumbent,
utter his first words; or Rosa Adkins,
the oracle at ninety-four,
reveal the secrets
of a long life.

Coming Down With Something

With only one child to go,
and being merely on a retainer
for the other three,
I look forward to becoming
a solo act.

Of course, it will mean
doing all the chores myself.
A small price, I say
for more elbow room,
control of the airwaves,
a monopoly on the newspaper crosswords,
and empty rooms to play in.

I'll be able to leave
the toilet door open,
be untidy
and fart with immunity.
As I take clean towels
from the hall cupboard
and glance across at the toys
I can feel a happy childhood
coming on. Any day now
I might get the Lego out.

Contact

When I see you, I know this
is a visit and not a dream
and that the message is for your mother.
You are a lad again;
your hair, its youthful brown.
You are tanned and healthy,
your liver restored.

Your attitude is that of a convert
and you are knuckling down.
You've learnt the error of your ways, you tell me,
and the physical work is making you strong.
You are happier, healthier
and wiser than you've ever been.
This is what you want me to tell her.

It's a tough one. Though I
wrote to her when I read the death notice,
I've not seen her for years. I try
to respect her wishes. Then…
I visit her birthplace on
the other side of the continent
and it's there I feel I can do it.
I write the postcard from Geraldton.
I've seen Paul, I tell her.
He's happy and well and
working hard in the spirit world.

I've no idea how she'll take it and I'm anxious.
But I must honour your wish
so I send it.

Chinese Translation

Far away from football
and a focus on the weather
my schedule is tight with
English classes for senior students
whose lives are leavened
by dreams of superstardom
and the promises of pop music.
Inside this oriental cocoon
their sights shift and sway
as tensions slap the sides
of a culture so old it slurs its speech.
In this garden of slim pickings
they embrace belief
and trust that a chance alchemy
will thrust them onto the path
of a ticket out
or an avalanche of opportunities
dense with distinction and exotic fruits,
subtle as background music,
thick with certainty
and, unmistakably,
playing their song.

Chronic Fatigue Syndrome

If sleep earns me anything at all,
I'm forced to spend the lot on waking up.
As I struggle from my dream
where I was paralysed and mute,
the thief demands everything I have
for consciousness.

Exhausted, I stagger into morning.
My day is spent
in the soup kitchen of my mind,
begging my strength.
I am thrifty.
I can't afford to answer the phone
or open the door to visitors.

At the supermarket I wear
sun glasses to say I'm closed.
In the car I chance it on
a pittance of concentration.
At the library I often pretend
to have means when I'm skint.
I hobo through my week
vagrant, destitute.

A two-year energy crisis with no relief
and this aching debit cancels all my interest.
You'll recover, the experts say,
in a year or two. Meanwhile,
the thief remains at large
practising the very worst
kind of extortion.

Cottesloe: An Impromptu for Carol Pettit

We walk the foreshore to the
breakwater and back
before fetching the picnic,
then sit close in shade,
our woman energy an exotic mix
turning heads like the scent of incense.

Our laughter floats like
painted opals on the breeze
drawing looks from the quietly envious
and the stubbornly staid.
Your sleek muscles shape the denim
of your jeans. My senses hug you.

Curled up beneath the trees
we embrace and laugh
about simple things;
our love, with its elegant feet,
dances, its long limbs slipping
sideways on the grass.

The amber flow of a discreet kiss
sheds its skin, and the earth tilts
to accommodate the lush audacity
of something god-like
to be its sacred self.

Father

As he asks my mother
if he should lower the hotplate
before lighting the barbecue
I wonder why, at seventy-eight,
he still asks the questions
when he knows the answers
will be humiliation, at best.

Later, to a captive audience
he raises his glass of port
and reminds my mother,
each time she says it will kill him,
that it's taking a bloody long time.

Over the years, he's shown traces
of an identity, but mostly he's
been a silent amusement piece.
When my mother pulls his string
he utters a predictable retort
from his small repertoire of responses
like Whatever you say, Clare, or
All complaints must be put in writing.

He's a peaceful man.
At the first hint of battle
he deserts to the casino
or the Marquis, on foot.
He returns as quietly as
he left, silent secret crusader
alive with potential.

But he'll never come out now.
His passions sleep too soundly
behind the black and white image
with the sound turned down
still operating on the original
set of instructions.

I often wonder if regret
colours his thoughts.
It's as if, long ago
he hung his personality
on a hook behind the door
and forgot where he put it.

Frail

Slippered feet shift fluff and vagrant dog hair
and brush aside dead flies with fractured wings.
He listens and musters will to hear where
the crickets chirrup and the blackbird sings.

Foaming springs of memory bubble up
and slide a smile t'wards weathered face and lips;
he reaches for his battered old tin cup
and checks the pain of both arthritic hips.

Small shapes of morning light tattoo the floor.
The warmth thaws out his ancient slippered toes.
His gaze flows out the window past the door,
alights upon a full-blown lilac rose.

Slow resignation settles in his head
and urges him to shuffle back to bed.

Golden but Tarnished

In vain I search for the adhesive
that's held them together for over fifty years.
A long run in anyone's language
even if their audience has fallen off.

They haven't changed their act much.
But since my father lost his voice
he can no longer do his standard jokes and so
spares my mother the humiliation.

The balance of power has swung her way
somewhat. His superior knowledge of everything
over the years has left him in diminished
health from malnutrition and alcohol abuse.

His university education and years spent
with mortar and pestle in his dispensary
gave him the edge then, and even after
retirement, but after their last move

he decided to sit out his life reading in his
favourite chair where a leg ulcer, pneumonia,
a thrombosis and a neglected skin cancer
have inconvenienced my mother no end.

He has ten years on her, but was in perfect
health until he decided he was old and
should do nothing. We encourage Mum
to threaten the nursing home when he's uncooperative.

When he last went to hospital you could
hear the relief in her voice. He was taking me down
with him, she said, shedding her burden. After she'd
go to visit him in the mornings she would defect

to the casino, and there she'd stay until it was
time to go back in the evening. She misses
her freedom. I could almost hear her disappointment
when she rang to tell me he was home again.

It's hard to say what's held them together
all these years. Probably just the glue of
expectation. Non-toxic, certainly, as they've come
to no real harm. But long term use caused
irritation and significantly stunted their growth.

Isobar Pearl

With the turn of each tide
she can read on the ripples
the shape of the relationship.

The space and isolation
surrounding this plinth
she recognises as hers.

Threaded, shining like nacre
on its invisible string,
its music pleases her.

The singing of the wind,
the inscrutable echo of the island
fills her with a primitive lust.

The breeze plays with her hair
as she throws her head back
and laughs in the knowledge
that this hypnotic place
questions not her presence
nor her right to remain.

Moon-faced she breathes lunar light,
burnished skies, brittle stars
and ice-rimmed rocks in winter.
Her frozen breath thaws to dew in spring.
The damp peels away old reticence
and leaves her poised on the edge of a new momentum.

Sea birds fly off in symbolic release.
A hint of ash settles on her skin.

It's a Small World

Rien ne va plus!
Rien ne va plus!
intoned the croupier
launching the tiny ball
into another lap of the wheel.

I savoured holding
my French Pacific Francs
and hummed into the excitement
of my long-coveted first trip
to a foreign land.
We took our time debating –
in English – a possible system.

Well, wadda ya know, Aussies!
jarred the voice from behind –
an obscene intrusion
on the sacred harmony
of my dreaming.
Where are yers from, he drawled,
I'm from Canberra!

Bleudi ockeur! we muttered
in our best French accents.

Knitting

Perhaps there was something
missing in my life.
My focus became feverish
my output fecund
as I had friends
save their bread bags
and began buying varieties
I'd never eaten before.
I was looking for colour.

With shredded plastic
and number eight needles
I click-teased the thread into shape
and bought wooden coat hangers
on the cheap in bulk
to wear the finished garment.
I stockpiled for school fairs
and gave them away to friends.
My ability to recognise
the transformed article
was my party piece.

An oversupply of white sliced
and wholemeal were snatched up
by the undiscriminating
while stone-ground and multigrain
drew the more discerning customer.
The prettiest colours,
Vogel, Fruit Loaf and Rye,
became collectors' items.

I basked in the attention
of a celebrated inventor,
the bread bag impresario
loving the spotlight.
In awe of this new hybrid
interested parties made their choices
from the available menu
as seriously as if the
plastic-covered hangers
themselves were fibre rich.

Menopause

1. The Onset

It's been a rough year.
Roll on menopause, I used to say.
Well it did.
Now I want it to roll off.

For back stiffness
I lie on the floor with
the egg timer
drawing in pelvic muscles
until the bell rings.

The new diet helps.
I wash down rice-oat muffins
with rosehip tea before bed
and rehearse breakfast
behind the falling curtain of sleep.

In the morning I awake
tormented by the unknowable.
In the shower I wrestle with lethargy
my dreams as dry as cuttlefish.
I've forgotten the alphabet
that made sense of my life.

For focus
and a period of purpose
I polish the silver.
Calm, connected
the cloth and I are one
moving like coconut palms
paying homage.

I bow before the altar of my relief.
The coffee spoons are candles.
Every fork a shrine.

2. The Treatment

I spend the summer in therapy
in my garden.
I rub out the weeds
counsel the soil
and question the bees with vehemence.
Under pressure
they spill their guts
and tell me everything.

I pine for peace
long for balance to return
and plant annuals
expecting them to last forever.
I'm not very well.

There is no rain
so I water within the restrictions
and weep copiously.
Things grow
as I struggle against wilt.
My landscape is parched.

I sweep up leaves
and spread them in the garden
on old newspapers
full of my past attention.
I want it back.

Tossed in the fluid rhythms
of breakthrough pleading
I steady my ship
and sail back into the chaos
to await my next session.

Mental Illness (Lisa unwell)

It's quite the saddest thing when it sets in:
The quiver in her voice, the slowing down,
the quiet separation; her hope so thin
she barely breathes while struggling not to drown
in this preface to the old vibration.
The invisible bombs shatter her still.
Thoughts flick by in snappy sensation,
disturb her sleep and paralyse her will.
This wasteland of slow returning winter
wipes her smiles. Dramatic paradoxes
prick her skin, sense and cohesion splinter,
firing shards as sharp as ears on foxes.
Her fragile balance barely holds beyond
her favourite yellow gerberas by the pond.

New Father, My Son

It's clear as he hugs me that
he's stuck in that male place
where emotions overwhelm
and boundaries still won't yield.
A long embrace, a few sob-like
gulps but no tears, then he
introduces me to his son.

The baby is snatched from
the current holder and
excitedly thrust at me:
Here he is, Mum. Isn't he beautiful?
My pleasure is untidy but
not as vagrant as my son's.
He's almost singing.
He hovers in my space,
his attention glued to my
face fixed on the baby's.

I want to examine the child –
relive precious memories.
I volunteer to change him.
There you go, Mum, says his father,
promptly laying down a plastic sheet.
This is nappy central. I place
the newborn on the bed and
together we carry out the task.

The baby looks nothing like him yet,
but he's a besotted parent and hasn't
left the hospital in four days.
At night he trundles out his
folding bed (from a cupboard
under the stairs) and sleeps
with the baby and its mother
wedged between the gifts and floral tributes.

In the voice he used
when he was twelve,
he shares with me the news
that the doctor allowed
him to deliver the baby:
I pulled him out, Mum, he
blurts in a staccato string,
awkwardly juggling his joy
and self-consciously spilling
a few drops of his
new personal worth.

The baby fusses at the breast –
can't get a grip. Just a minute,
says his father, and pops his little
finger into the baby's mouth.
Contact with the top palate engages
the sucking reflex, he informs me,
as the baby sucks with increasing
vigour. When he judges the moment
to be right, he deftly substitutes nipple
for finger and the baby's away.

I find the whole
experience overwhelming;
this boy/man
caught in the light,
the casual nod of Providence
throwing him something new.
I watch him hold back ghosts
while beckoning a new belief,
and from some empty space
he retrieves a sequence that he
hopes will see him safely through
the rituals and routines
where a lingering sweetness
will stay switched on like the sun.

His life grows larger.
He keeps his finger on the pulse,
checks the balance of things,
concentrates on specifications
and baby acumen,
and the habit of sanctuary
forms round him
like skin.

Nullarbor Cathedral

No Sistine ceiling in this deep space,
just pristine blue dome
with no art work more imaginative than clouds.

Emus instead of pews
run across the open-plan sanctuary,
its congregation, people on the move
but always with time
for a waved greeting of peace.

No bell tower rings out the hour
or the occasion
but a steady procession of believers
down the longest aisle
is music enough.

Pieces of stained glass
glint in the sunlight.
The landscape gives up its earthy incense.
At night stars light up a vast altar.

A three-day benediction
in this sacred isolation,
another country,
where flat earth theory is gospel
every soul redeemed
and goodwill the standard offering.

Out here
there are no philistines
and everyone speaks Greek.

Opinion Poll

I sometimes wonder if I'm the only one
unable to take politicians seriously.
When I catch a glimpse of parliamentary
sessions on the TV news, it reminds me
of unruly schoolboy debates
rank with posturing,
chaired by someone
unable to keep order.

When my children reached voting age
and asked my advice on choosing a candidate
I told them I attempt to sift through the election
promises, looking for a grain of credibility.
If this proves fruitless, I weigh up
the names at heart level
hoping for a revelation.
If all else fails
I look away
and pin the tail on the donkey.

Outback

(after Russell Drysdale)

The horizon and russet ranges ring
the chestnut landscape, rough, tinged with a boat–
like boldness and solidity, a thing
of bruised colour, a copper sky. Birds float
on absolute silence. Thin shadows in
trance-like shapes, red earth and boulders, crave shade.
A strange illusion sits like light on skin,
more apparition than real, like brown suede.
At night, you look at stars and dream a beach,
wet with alien shine stretching to blue
sky, tall trees, grass and coolness within reach,
then wake to this untrammelled space where you
watch dust, wood smoke and ashes cast a band
dense with myth and fresh clues across the land.

Pirates Bay

for Colin Knight

The black and white snapshot
fills the picture-window frame.
From a dark
and sullen sea
waves in tantrums
throw themselves down
on the sand.
The jagged cliff face
frowns
at the white caps
of the ocean's spleen.
Water rushes up
into crevices,
spray explodes
over the rocky shelf
like spilt milk.

The landscape's expression
is peevish.
The horizon sulks
behind a hostile blur.

Plastic

They used to make flowers out of it,
coat hangers, hair rollers,
shower curtains, swimming pools,
drinking straws and baby strollers.

They put food in large transparent bags of it.
Make busts of Mozart and shopping tags of it.
It waterproofs beds and makes beer cans a set.
It litters beaches, chokes penguins and stops people getting wet.

It makes fibre and fabric for pantyhose and drapes,
children's tents, beach balls, masks and Batman capes.
Seaweed imitates it, spiders' webs and garden slugs,
it covers books, lines garbage bins, makes picture frames and bath plugs.

Even cars are largely made of it nowadays.
But its best incarnation was the artificial flower days.

Recycled

As I sift through the offerings
of the careers guide weighing up
the jobs from A–Z wondering
what I'll do when the pension
stops, the excitement of the
challenge and the sting of
the insult irritate me.

No retirement plan for mothers
means no-one appreciates
a good juggling act anymore.
As I apply myself to the F jobs
the children encourage me:
What are you going to be
this week, Mum, a fireman?

Many times I've been
a calculator and the
home reference library
while holding down a dozen
other jobs but there was never
any pay or recognition.

The children are optimistic.
They look on proudly as I
lose myself in the great big
adventure book for finished
mums and wonder what I'll
be when they grow up.

Rainy Day Sonnet

The damp peers in through dirty window panes.
The power lines wear strings of pearl-like drips
from summer showers of drought relieving rains,
thanksgiving prayers on everybody's lips.
Beyond the bank the river takes its fill
while vacant mist floats down to render faint
the distant hills and houses and old mill,
the fences, sheds and barns all needing paint.
The sound of rain is easy, hushed but clear.
It ushers in a sense of calm and peace
that all is well to end this dry old year,
that things will grow again and worries cease.
Outside my door the honeyeaters see
rain-glitter sparkle on their favourite tree.

Resurrection

My eldest rings from Perth.
She's resigned her job and
looking for a new one.
She's finished with the
psychologist and off
the Prozac. Her friends
are being supportive.
She's optimistic about the future.

The second one rings in crisis.
She's enjoying the DipEd
but can't handle the prac.
The students are rude.
The teachers encourage it.
Every kid in grade seven
has a laptop.
She doesn't want to be
a teacher anyway.

The third one rings
from up north.
He's alive and well.
Had his first Hydro bill.
A bit of a shock to the system.
His youth project
made the *Examiner* and his
flatmate's working out well.
He'll be home for Easter.

The youngest one comes in
and says someone stole
her hot cross buns from
the oven at school.
She's pretty peeved.
But life goes on.
Besides, she's in love.

Bless me father for
I have dreamed.
It's been twenty-five years.
Tomorrow's Good Friday.
I'm off to the shack
to lie low
and polish up my calm.
On the third day
I'll rise again.

Seeing Sam

This new relationship has a stark shine,
an ostentatious aura, expanding walls
and see-through skin, textured like muslin,
the fabric delicate, strong, precise.

White water pleasure rushes through me,
explodes my passion, my joy so sharp
it's painful. With wild and vivid lightness
I inhale his scent of newness and sigh

over fresh linen and the purity of new life
then bow before the coastline of this
connection in a sea of spreading wonder
on a rising swell of devotion.

Speaking With Picasso About His Work

1. The Artist's Mother (1896)

This pastel of your mother – a vital,
strong character, a unifying force –
is remarkable. The simple title,
this small, dark woman, sturdy, and, of course,
the one you most resembled; your father,
well-meaning but weak, mediocre as
a painter, an embarrassment. Rather
than use his name, you took hers. This fact has
been diversely interpreted; but you,
yourself, claimed it was simply because it
was striking and unusual. You drew
her quiet strength, her energy. Did she sit
for you? You've caught the maternal, serene;
her accomplished artist at just fifteen.

2. Old Jew with a Boy (1903)

White, claw-like skeletal bones aglow with
emaciation and blue light. Pale-faced,
seated close, sad, they contemplate the myth
of kindness to the wretched, poor, displaced;
the boy staring, the old man with no eyes.
Steeped in melancholy, cold, rejected
one assumes, this doomed tableau occupies
a space where nothing more seems expected.
These beggars people the canvas; outcasts,
but working here to amplify the theme
of pauper – that destitution outlasts
the lure of even the most humble dream.
Premeditated reflection on lack
compels your brush to hold the colour back.

3. Les Demoiselles d'Avignon (1907)

These aggressive distortions of truth shake
up the Paris art world. You somehow knew
this launched the revolt, a palpable break
with Western visual conventions few
would have challenged. Viewpoints and perspectives
are violated – figures seen from full
face and behind at once. This daring gives
a hint of your cubist future. Your pull
towards geometric shapes is showing.
Segments of colour mould these naked sprites,
their mask-like faces; earthy tones growing
in attitude and ugliness, your sights
set on change. Splendid curator of form,
poised, on the brink of unleashing a storm.

4. The Studio (1928)

Your genius here is revelling in its
total lack of subject. Having a go,
were you, at Mondrian's colourful fits
of flat, bright, geometric shapes? Your low –
density slim-line play, mere suggestion;
your brush, a single diagonal line;
your easel, a small circle; the question,
then, is where are you? Understated, fine
virtuoso work, a matching of strengths
with the Dutchman's abstract style, your wire
sculptures, an influence; the covert lengths
you went to, none too subtle. The fire
in your intent turns up your private joke –
you, in your studio, one artful stroke.

5. Weeping Woman (1937)

Intensely sad, this woman, her teeth bared,
devastated by shock, unhinged by pain,
chic Parisienne dame. She deeply cared
that little would remain of Guernica
after the bombing. She bellows her grief,
chews her hanky between teeth clenched in rage.
Sharp edges, shaped like shards, give some relief.
Her geometric breakdown on the page
reverberates with sobbing, her madness
emphasised by the smart red hat tipping.
Her eyes seem to separate with sadness,
her finger nails rubbed brittle with gripping
the news. You wanted to paint her shattered.
To you, her weeping was all that mattered.

Spirited Child

Thomas learned to play
'Chariots of Fire' on the organ.
He bounced his basketball around
the kitchen floor at tea time.
He practised tennis volleys on
his bedroom wall at bedtime.
He decorated his room
with pictures of
Frankenstein and Rambo.
Thomas was hit by a car
when he was only nine and
took his mother's advice
as he struggled by the roadside
and went towards the light.

His classmates carried him
into the church
in a small white box.
The organ paced its way
through 'Chariots of Fire'.
His family carried flowers and
his well-thumbed children's Bible.
His mother smiled but
had tears in her voice as
she stood at the church door
afterwards and thanked
each person for coming.

Thomas,
the boisterous boy who was rarely still,
waited patiently outside.

Spring Sonnet

The breeze licks my ears, soft-tickles my nose,
I fall for this seduction every time.
The soil I stand in plays between my toes,
adjacent bluebells watch the jasmine climb.
Colour stirs an earthy audacious scene
exploding palettes, releasing washes
of contrasting tones to dress up plump green
succulents growing in old galoshes.
Perfume rides the breeze, new fragrances split
open in the warm earth's concentration.
Birds speak fluent spring, deft butterflies flit,
wing-beats dance a carnal celebration.
At dusk I stand transfixed in mauve half-light,
and watch the day drift off into the night.

Strained

When I was crazy
I'd get in my husband's car
teeth clenched, white knuckles gripping the wheel
and promise to drive into
the next telegraph pole.

Then I'd see visions of my four children
and let that one pass
but vow to hit the next one.

Skin and bone, I gave up on suicide
and maimed my left hand instead,
four times in the car door,
then I finally broke it with a beer bottle.

That eased my pain considerably.
At the clinic I watched others
tear up pillow slips
and stab cardboard boxes
and I felt I was winning the battle.

In week four I realised
my shrink had more problems
than I did and I began
to counsel myself.
My progress was rapid.

Being loony was safe and stress-free.
If it hadn't been for the children
I'd never have given it up.

The Birthday Party

Inside the ranting raw nerve of a woman
a serene soul
waits patiently for recognition.

Meanwhile she's bent on perfection.
With every detail of the day choreographed
the first domino falls as guests arrive.

Seven months pregnant
she reverberates through her blueprint
for the tightly strung afternoon.

Her momentum ignited
and intoxicated by her own delirium
she topples the day into vertigo.

Someone lights the fire a moment too soon.
Her invective poisons the air.
Guests hold their breath.

Lethal with purpose
she directs the gathering of two-year-olds
irritated things aren't going to plan.

Distressed by the sabotage
she lashes out at bystanders
desperate to finger a culprit.

Stripped of all comfort
the wounded gather on their marks
a clean getaway their sole objective.

The kookaburras

know she's here. They're laughing.
It's her sixteenth coming. She chooses her
site for privacy and pitches her tent
by the creek
and the sound of running water.

In the afternoon she writes.
Every imaginable insect visits her page.
Some red, and no bigger than a full stop.
Three black and amber butterflies,

celebrating her presence, fly healing
circles inside her open tent.
They alight close up and stay long
enough to dazzle her with their wing art.

Against the tinkling of the water
blowflies practise low flying, their
harmonies close and discordant. Like
oil paint, her contentment extrudes

itself onto the slow momentum of her day.
Intimacies seep from blue sky
along low-lying cloud
to crisp sheets of water
where everything feels horizontal.

The Tao of Loss

Even an abstract mindset
won't hold the canvas still.
I finally caught up with her
eating grapes outside the supermarket.
It's four months since the child died.
In typically comic mode she said
nursing that kid was the hardest thing
she's ever done. She threw the
grape seeds into the ether as we talked.

The artist leans wildly into the work
looking for meaning.
She told me of the trip from
death's threshold in the Whittle Ward
direct to Myer because T-shirts were
on special and the kid wanted
to do her shopping since it now
looked like she'd see Christmas.

Beyond the horizon float watermelon
dreams and coloured stars.
I could see six years of exhaustion
in her face. She had the flu –
time at last to be sick.
She misses the child, she said,
but dislikes having the grave
and wants to know where she really is.
Grape pips fly over her shoulder.
Her former belief system's crap now, she said.

Blended memories tumble in
and blow restless across the landscape.
Our paths have diverged since the early days.
She's still the consummate eccentric.
Laughing was always what we did best.
Even in grief she has life on a string.
Her agony is illusive and intangible,
dim and shadowy,
with almost an oriental flavour.
It reminds me of the time she came to the party
wearing chopsticks in her hair.

Then Let Her Slip Away

You're always in red when I see you.
You wind me up
then have to go somewhere
but return and pull my strings.
It was better than that in real life.
Eight years of magnetic coupling.
Looks at first
then up the scale from
careful to pressing exchanges
caught clusters of all our obsession craved.
We eclipsed our own fears
and others' worst suspicions.
In those hours stolen from
household chores and children
we were innocents ourselves
lurching in a landscape
that overwhelmed us.
Twelve years since I've seen you
and I can't break the habit.
Memory rings sweet
like the songs we sang.
Images sprawl like we did.
We were sunlight on water, fathoms deep.
Now I only see you in my dreams
an almanac of raw resonance
and illicit rainbows.
Keep on surfacing
if only as the apotheosis of the no longer attainable
to remind me how rich
I once was.

Tissue Test

Even in other people's houses
I sometimes change
the toilet roll around
so it feeds out from the top
making access easier.

I often wonder if they notice
after I've gone.
Or maybe change it back
because they, too,
have the same obsession in reverse.

With a mixture of guilt
that I'm overstepping the line
and relief that I'm
keeping my world in order,
I wonder why the best way
isn't obvious to everyone.

While it's not premeditated –
when I'm on the spot
I can't resist the temptation.
I crusade secretly,
proud to be setting the right example.

I am passionate about my mission.
And in spite of what
the cosmologists say,
when I'm liberating the two-ply,
I know with conviction
I am more than stardust.

Tom

This slip of a boy-child tips his world
grips his calves, looks backwards
thinks and blinks in the glare
spins and grins and bares his tongue
spittle-pink and starboard-curled;
he sometimes sees angels.

He fans life back into fading moments,
stands the moon on its head,
scatters the doves to assert his power
and independence, his momentum
a consummate cakewalk across
the delicate stage of his routine
before the climax of his day falls silent
to meet the early rising decibels
heralding his firm grip on the next.

Tryst

The rocking of the van heightens the pleasure.
I move my tongue round
the curve of the pinkish mound,
the soft cool surface,
eyes closed in concentration.

Gusts of wind blow rice paper leaves
from branches already thinning
in their autumn imperative,
the grey pockmarked limbs
leaning out over the sloping bank
to dwell on their reflection.

I try to sustain the moment,
lick and suck in a rhythm.
The wind whips up stronger now
my tongue works in anticipation
of the end, the resignation, the afterglow.

The river surface ripples
in a shiver of response.
A mother duck and her chicks
as if momentarily disoriented
wander aimlessly amongst the reeds.

It's getting late.
I reflect on the sweetness of the encounter,
the sensual indulgence,
the simplicity of my delight,
sticky fingers, round a waffle cone,
a liaison I like to keep secret.

Valediction

I've joined the doll's house in the back room
to sleep in the beds and ride on the dreams of my children.
It's easier there to share with the house
the memories of twenty-five years.
I conjure up visions of hairspray being applied
in the crush for a final check at the mirror
before the dash for the door to catch the bus,
the poster of Cat Stevens smiling down
as the stampede descends the stairs
and goodbyes drift back
heralding the final door slam.

The history of their tenure is recorded in every stain,
every wallpaper tear
and secret writing under window sills
now dispossessed of its proud artisans.
I regularly send them fan mail
and urge them to ply the trade I taught them
when we dared to be different in this house of revolution
where butterflies fanned our psyches
and laughter oiled every cog.
Reminiscences peel off every surface like old paint.

This house has counselled me through grief,
embraced me through loneliness,
rocked with me in celebration.
It proudly wore the children's artistic efforts on its walls
long after they had left home,
then shared with me a growing longing
for a less serious existence.
I've loved this relationship –
I knew every door-creak and footfall.

Now I want to lie back in the
grooves the children occupied,
lie fallow in the furrows of time
and prepare to take my leave.
But not before I climb into the lap of every room,
feel the full embrace of a passionate past,
hear the muted music of Matchbox cars and marbles,
and hold the memory of little hands
that will cling to mine
as I bravely walk away.

Villanelle for the Scotsman

The Scotsman had his llama on a lead.
With tartan beret propped complete with feather
he settled in for coffee and a feed.

He looked a fairly unfamiliar breed
and didn't seem concerned about the weather
the Scotsman had his llama on a lead.

Perhaps he followed some alternate creed
his woolly pet and him always together
he settled in for coffee and a feed.

He didn't seem the type to harbour greed
his pet relaxed, not bother by his tether.
The Scotsman had his llama on a lead.

If strangers look askance he paid no heed
he chatted to a friend and gripped the leather.
He settled in for coffee and a feed.

It's hard to know if ever he had need
to think about his land of heath and heather,
the Scotsman had his llama on a lead,
he settled in for coffee and a feed.

Wheels of Fortune

Bikes in China, like shrubs and trees, are part
of the landscape. They flow thickly along
bitumen arteries out from the heart
of a city. The ancient frames wince, strong
but black with age. They pivot over rough
terrain, heavy with produce; this hauling,
a daily challenge to build up enough
momentum to keep the load from falling.
Sometimes they carry children sitting staid
and passive behind; or sleeping babes slumped
like broken dolls in wicker seats not made
to last. Late in the day this stream is pumped
in the other direction. As light fails
they rattle home like treasured rusty nails.

www.ingramcontent.com/pod-product-compliance
Ingram Content Group UK Ltd.
Pitfield, Milton Keynes, MK11 3LW, UK
UKHW022209230426
12048UKWH00016BA/739